The Believer's Secret of the Abiding Presence

The Believer's Secret of the Abiding Presence

Compiled from the writings of

Andrew Murray
Brother Lawrence

by Louis Gifford Parkhurst Jr.

BETHANY HOUSE PUBLISHERS
MINNEAPOLIS, MINNESOTA 55438
A Division of Bethany Fellowship, Inc.

Unless otherwise indicated, the Scripture quotations in this book are from the Holy Bible: New International Version. Copyright © 1978 by the New York International Bible Society. Used by permission of Zondervan Bible Publishers.

Published by Bethany House Publishers
A Division of Bethany Fellowship, Inc.
6820 Auto Club Road, Minneapolis, Minnesota 55438

Printed in the United States of America

Library of Congress Cataloging-in-Publication Data

Parkhurst, Louis Gifford, 1946-
The believer's secret of the abiding presence.

Includes a modernization of Murray's The secret of the abiding presence and a rewriting of Lawrence's The practice of the presence of God.

1. Mystical union—Meditations. 2. God—Omnipresence—Meditations. I. Murray, Andrew, 1828-1917. Secret of the abiding presence. II. Lawrence, of the Resurrection, Brother, 1611-1691. Pratique de la présence de Dieu. III. Title.
BT767.7.P37 1986 231.7 86-28307
ISBN 0-87123-899-3

This book is dedicated to the staff and students of Bethany Fellowship and Bethany House Publishers; especially to Gary and Carol Johnson, and Nathan Unseth, who labor with the Lord to spread His Gospel around the world.

Andrew Murray

Andrew Murray was born in South Africa in 1828. After receiving his education in Scotland and Holland, he returned to that land and spent many years there as both pastor and missionary. He was a staunch advocate of biblical Christianity. He is best known for his many devotional books.

Brother Lawrence

Brother Lawrence was born in Lorraine, France, as Nicholas Herman. At middle age, he became a lay brother in the Order of the Carmelites. His thoughts on the presence of God were collected and published by Abbe' Joseph De Beaufort. He was a monastery cook, who died in 1691, near the age of eighty. His approach to God was through Christ in love and faith.

L. G. Parkhurst, Jr.

L. G. Parkhurst, Jr., is the pastor of the First Christian Church of Rochester, Minnesota. He has compiled and edited several volumes of the writings of Charles G. Finney for Bethany House Publishers.

Contents

Preface

After Jesus sent the Holy Spirit into the hearts of His disciples on the day of Pentecost, we find no record of them ever regretting the absence of the physical presence of Jesus. They had nothing to regret, because He was present with them through the power and presence of the Holy Spirit in their lives. Wherever they were, whether together in Jerusalem or scattered about in various parts of the world on their missionary tours, Christ was present with each one of them personally and individually.

Jesus has promised us exactly what we find in the lives of His first disciples: His very presence empowering us to live the Christian life. Andrew Murray recognized "the failure of the church as a whole to enter experientially into the abundance of the life that is in Christ, and to teach definitely the fullness of His power to redeem and to save. The Church must stand with a more triumphant gospel if the dead weight of dullness and unspirituality, of unbelief and heathen tradition is to be lifted from the Church. The tides would surely run more strongly if the church as a whole had a firmer and clearer faith in God, who, as revealed in the New Testament, is overflowingly alive." To remedy this problem, and to teach us how to know Jesus Christ personally and experientially, Murray wrote *The Secret of the Abiding Presence.*

About 200 years before Murray wrote his book, a

poor monk in France, Brother Lawrence, discovered that our supreme purpose in life is to have a conscious, personal union with God in Christ through faith. Brother Lawrence's life was so remarkable that following his death some of his conversations and letters were collected and published as *The Practice of the Presence of God.*

The Believer's Secret of the Abiding Presence combines these two great classics from Andrew Murray and Brother Lawrence. The language of both has been modernized, but the style of Lawrence's book is so antiquated that I have rewritten his conversations and letters as personalized principles that we can consciously and prayerfully apply. With Andrew Murray's inspiring devotionals, we are presenting Brother Lawrence's ideas with a view to practical application. I have added a brief prayer of my own, which I hope will encourage you to pray your own prayer and practice the presence of Christ in your own life. Finally, I have used the text of the New International Version of the Bible.

I wish to give my sincere thanks to Nathan Unseth, Assistant Editor, of Bethany House Publishers for suggesting this project. His assistance and initial labor was vital, and I appreciate his encouragement in a project he had thought about for quite some time. To further pursue the ideas in this book, I recommend the devotional by Charles G. Finney, *Principles of Union with Christ*, also published by Bethany House Publishers.

For the sake of His Kingdom,
L. G. Parkhurst, Jr.

And surely I will be with you always, to the very end of the age.

Matthew 28:20

1
The Abiding Presence

The Lord chose His twelve disciples "that they might be with him and that he might send them out to preach" (Mark 3:14). His earthly fellowship with them would prepare and fit them for the work of preaching.

The disciples were so deeply conscious of their great privilege in knowing Jesus that when He spoke of leaving them to go to the Father, their hearts were filled with great sorrow. The presence of Christ had become indispensable to them. They could not think of living without Him.

To comfort the disciples, Christ gave them the promise of the Holy Spirit, with the assurance that they would then have Him (Christ himself) in His heavenly presence in a sense far deeper and more intimate than they had ever known on earth. The law of their first vocation remained unchanged: being with Him, living in unbroken fellowship with Him, would give them the secret power by which they would preach and tell others about Him.

When Christ gave them the Great Commission to go into all the world and to preach the gospel to every creature, He added the words: "*And surely I will be with you always, to the very end of the age*" (Matt. 28:20).

For all time, this principle remains valid for all His servants. Without the experience of His presence always abiding with them, their preaching will have no power. The secret of their effectiveness will be the living demonstration that Jesus Christ is with them every moment, inspiring, directing, and strengthening them. The presence of Christ will enable His followers to boldly preach Him as the crucified One in the midst of His enemies.

The early disciples never for a moment regretted His bodily absence. They had Him with them, and in them, in the divine power of the Holy Spirit.

Through a living faith, the Christian's success in his work depends upon his consciousness of the abiding presence of the Lord Jesus with him. An essential element in the preaching of the gospel is a living experience of the presence of Jesus in our lives. If our experience of His presence is clouded, then our work will become a human effort, without the freshness and the power of the heavenly life. Nothing can bring back the power and the blessing Jesus promised except a return to the feet of the Master; there He breathes into the heart, in divine power, His blessed word: "And surely I will be with you always!"

The Practice of the Presence of God

Establish a sense of God's presence in your life by continually conversing with Him. Do not quit conversing with Him to think of *trifling* and foolish things.

Nourish yourself with high conceptions of God, which shall bring you great joy in being devoted to Him.

Quicken your faith. Instead of taking faith as the rule of your conduct, you may be just amusing yourself with trivial acts of devotion which change daily. The way of faith is the spirit of the church, and faith is sufficient to bring you to a high degree of perfection.

Give yourself to God with regard to things both temporal and spiritual. Seek your satisfaction only in the fulfilling of His will, whether He leads you by suffering or by consolation; for either would be equal to a person truly committed and submitted to His will.

Establish your loyalty to God by your fidelity in prayer even in those times of dryness or sluggishness or weariness by which God tries your love for Him. Times of dryness are the times for you to make good and effective acts of commitment and submission. In fact, one act alone will very often promote your spiritual advancement greatly.

*D*ear Jesus, thank you for promising your heavenly presence in the lives of your devoted disciples. Today, I renew my vow of loyalty to you, and I thank you for being as faithful to me as you have been to all your followers. Alert me when I stray from your presence. Call me back when I wander from your will. Remind me to come back and fall at your feet again should my relationship with you become clouded by any unfaithfulness. May the words of your faithful servants of the past encourage me daily. Amen.

All authority [power, KJV] in heaven and on earth has been given to me.

Matthew 28:18

2 The Omnipotence of Christ

Before Christ gave His disciples their Great Commission to begin that great world conquest of bringing His gospel to every creature, He first revealed himself in His divine power as a partner with God himself, the Almighty One. Their faith in His divine power enabled them to undertake their work in all simplicity and boldness. After they began to know Him in the mighty resurrection power that had conquered sin and death, there was nothing too great for Him to command or for them to undertake.

Every disciple of Jesus Christ should desire to take part in the victory that overcomes the world. But, in addition to desire, he will need time, faith, and the Holy Spirit in order to come under the full conviction that he is to take his part in the work as the *servant* of the omnipotent Lord Jesus. He is to literally count upon the daily experience of being "strong in the Lord and in his mighty power" (Eph. 6:10). The word of promise gives the courage to obey implicitly the word of command.

Just think of the power of Jesus Christ that the disciples came to know here on earth. And yet that power was but a little thing when compared to the greater works that He was now to do in and through them. Jesus has the power to work with the strength of Almighty God in His most feeble servants. He even has the power to use their apparent weakness to carry out His purposes. He has power over every enemy, every human heart, and every difficulty and danger.

But remember: Jesus never meant His power to be experienced as though it were our own. Only as Jesus Christ, as a living Person, dwells and works with His divine energy in our own heart and life can we have power in our witnessing as a personal demonstration. Only after Christ had said to Paul, "My power is made perfect in weakness," could Paul say (what he had never learned to say before), "When I am weak, then I am strong" (2 Cor. 12:9, 10). Only the disciple of Christ rightly understands that all His power has been entrusted to him, to be received hour by hour from Christ. The disciple of Christ will feel the need of His power, and experience the power of that precious word: "And surely I will be with you always"—I, the Almighty One.

The Practice of the Presence of God

We hear daily about sin and misery in the world, but we should be surprised that there is not more, considering the malice sinners are capable of perpetrating. You must pray for them, but do not worry and fret since you know that God can remedy the mischief.

To arrive at the submission God requires, watch attentively over all your passions and emotions—especially over those that mingle with your spiritual life. God will give you light regarding these if you truly desire to serve Him.

You must always be governed by love, without selfish views. You must resolve to make the love of God the end or purpose of all your actions. Learn to pick up even a straw from the ground for the love of God, seeking Him only and nothing else—not even His gifts.

Resolve: "I will engage in a religious life only for the love of God; and I will endeavor to act only for Him; whatever becomes of me I will always continue to act purely for the love of God."

Do not place your sins between God and you! Place your faith in Christ as your Savior. Do not put your faith in yourself or in your actions, but in Christ, and you will pass your life in perfect liberty and continual joy.

*D*ear Father, I pray to you in the name of your dear Son Jesus Christ, and I confess my sins to you and ask for your forgiveness through His death upon the cross in my behalf. I love you and long to serve you with the best of my ability, but my ability is as nothing compared to your great power. The great need for the gospel in our world overwhelms me. Oh, give me your strength and power, love through me, that I might do all for you and others to the glory of your kingdom and your name. Amen.

I will be with you.

Exodus 3:12

3
The Omnipresence of Christ

When man first conceives of a god, his first thought is that of power, however limited. The first thought of the true God is of His omnipotence: "I am God Almighty." The second thought in Scripture is of His omnipresence. God always gave His servants the promise of His unseen presence with them. To His "I will be with you," their faith responded: "You are with me."

When Christ said to His disciples, "All authority [power] in heaven and on earth has been given to me," the promise immediately followed, "And surely I will be with you always." The omnipotent One is surely the omnipresent One.

The Psalmist speaks of God's omnipresence as something beyond his comprehension: "Such knowledge is too wonderful for me, too lofty for me to attain" (Ps. 139:6).

The revelation of God's omnipresence in the man Christ Jesus makes the mystery still deeper. The grace that enables us to claim this presence as our strength and our joy is something inexpressibly blessed. And yet when the promise is given to them, how many servants of Christ find it difficult to understand all that is implied in it—and how it can become the practical experience of their daily lives.

Here, as elsewhere in the spiritual life, everything depends upon our faith accepting Christ's word as a divine reality, and trusting the Holy Spirit to make it true to us from moment to moment. When Christ says "always" (Greek: "all the days"), He means to give us the assurance that we are not to have a day of our lives in which His blessed presence is not to be with us. And "all the days" implies "all the day." There need not be a moment in which that presence cannot be our experience. It does not depend upon what we can effect, but upon what He undertakes to do. The omnipotent Christ is the omnipresent Christ; the ever-present is the everlasting, the unchangeable One. Just as surely as He is the unchangeable One who has the power of an endless life will His presence be with each of His servants who trusts Him for it.

Our attitude must be that of a quiet, restful faith, of a humble, lowly dependence in accordance with the Word: "Be still before the Lord and wait patiently for him" (Ps. 37:7).

"And surely I will be with you always." Let your faith in Christ, the omnipresent One, be in the quiet confidence that He will every day and every moment keep you as the apple of His eye, keep you in perfect peace and in the sure experience of all the light and the strength you need in His service.

The Practice of the Presence of God

In order to form a habit of conversing with God continually, and referring all you do to Him, you must at first apply your prayers to Him with some diligence. But after that, you should find that His love inwardly excites you to conversation without any difficulty.

After the pleasant days God has given you, if you ever have pain or suffering, do not be uneasy about it, knowing that God will give you strength to bear it.

When you are practicing a particular virtue, address yourself to God, praying, "Lord, I cannot do this unless you enable me," and you shall receive His strength more than sufficiently for your needs.

If you should fail in your duty, confess your fault to God and pray, "I shall always fail if you leave me to myself; hinder my falling and mend whatever is missing in my life."

You ought to act with God in the greatest simplicity. Speak to Him frankly and plainly. Implore His assistance in your affairs just as they are happening: He will never fail to grant it.

*D*ear Father God, thank you for your love and strength that sustains me each moment of the day. I pray that your Holy Spirit would make your presence and the presence of your Son known to me in a deeper and more personal way than I have ever known before. I am not praying for an occasional spiritual high, but I am humbly asking you to help me be more aware of you every moment of the day. Amen.

They said to the woman, "We no longer believe just because of what you said; now we have heard for ourselves, and we know that this man really is the Savior of the world."

John 4:42

4
Christ the Savior of the World

Omnipotence and omnipresence are called natural attributes of God. They have their true worth only when linked to and inspired by His moral attributes: holiness and love. When our Lord spoke of omnipotence (all power on earth and in heaven) having been given to Him and His omnipresence (His presence with each of His disciples), His words pointed to that which lies at the root of all—His divine glory as the Savior of the world and Redeemer of men.

Because He humbled himself and became obedient to death, the death of the cross, God highly exalted Him. His share as the man Christ Jesus in the attributes of God was due to the work He did in His perfect obedience to the will of God and the finished redemption He wrought for the salvation of men.

His work of redemption gives meaning and worth to what He says about himself as the omnipotent and omnipresent One. Between His mention of these two attributes,

He gives His command that they should go out into all the world and preach the gospel, and teach people to obey all that He has commanded. As the Redeemer who saves and keeps from sin, the Lord Jesus expects obedience to all that He has commanded, and He promises that His divine presence will be with His servants.

It follows as a matter of necessity that only when His servants by their lives show that they obey Him in all His commands can they expect the fullness of His power and His presence to be with them. Only when they are living witnesses to the reality of His power to save and to keep from sin can they expect the full experience of His abiding presence. Then they will have power to train others to the life of obedience that He asks.

Yes, Jesus Christ, who saves His people from their sin, in the day of His power rules over a willing people and enables them to say, "To do your will, O my God, is my desire [delight, KJV]; your law is within my heart" (Ps. 40:8). The abiding presence of the Savior from sin is promised to all who have accepted Him in the fullness of His redeeming power, and who preach by their lives as well as by their words what a wonderful Savior He is.

The Practice of the Presence of God

If you must attend to any unpleasant business, or if a physical handicap inhibits your business ventures, do not be uneasy about it if your business is within the Lord's will. Say to God, "I will be about your business, and with your help I will perform it well."

Accustom yourself to do everything for the love of God, with prayer upon all occasions for His grace to do His work well, and you will find that the work you naturally have a great aversion to will be easy.

By doing even little things for the love of God, you will find yourself pleasing yourself and enjoying the task!

When your greatest business does not divert you from God, then times you have reserved for prayer will not be much different from other times. You will be conscious of a close relationship with God at all times.

When you are very conscious of your faults, do not be discouraged by them, but confess them to God. Do not excuse them, or accuse Him. Then, peaceably resume your usual practice of love and adoration of God.

*D*ear God, show me any sins that I may be committing unawares. Help me to forsake them immediately, and by the power of your Holy Spirit break the strong hold of their temptations. I desire to do your will; please give me the strength to forsake any sins which have become habits and to which I feel in bondage. Father, you know there are times that I must concentrate totally on a task and cannot be in conscious thought of you, but in those times I thank you for your presence and your guidance in fulfilling my responsibilities. By the gentle nudge of your Spirit, call me once again to prayer that I might do every task seeking your power and insight, and conscious that you are an ever present help in time of trouble. I love you, Father, and want to do everything for your ultimate glory. Amen.

May I never boast except in the cross of our Lord Jesus Christ, through which the world has been crucified to me, and I to the world.

Galatians 6:14

5
Christ Crucified

Christ's highest glory is His cross. On the cross He glorified His Father, and the Father glorified Him. The Lamb slain in the midst of the throne, described in the fifth chapter of Revelation, receives the worship of the ransomed, the angels, and all of creation. As the crucified One, His servants learned to say, "May I never boast except in the cross of our Lord Jesus Christ, through which the world has been crucified to me, and I to the world" (Gal. 6:14). Christ's highest glory should be our only glory too.

When the Lord Jesus said to His disciples, "And surely I will be with you always," it was as the crucified One that He gave them the promise, even as He showed them the cruel marks on His hands and His feet. Each one who seeks to claim the promise must realize: "It is the crucified Jesus who promises, who offers, to be with me every day."

Is this one reason we find it so difficult to expect and enjoy the abiding presence of Jesus Christ? Do we refuse to glory in the cross by which we are to be crucified to the world? We have been crucified with Christ: our old self was crucified with Him. You "who belong to Christ Jesus have crucified the sinful nature (flesh, KJV) with its passions and desires" (Gal. 6:24). And yet, how little we have learned that the world has been crucified to us, and that we are free from its power. As those who are crucified with Christ, how little we have learned to deny ourselves, to have the mind that was in Christ when He emptied himself and took the form of a servant, and humbled himself and became obedient even to the death on the cross.

Oh, let us learn the lesson! The crucified Christ is the One who comes to walk with us every day, and in whose power we too are to live the life that can say, "I have been crucified with Christ and I no longer live, but Christ lives in me" (Gal. 2:20).

The Practice of the Presence of God

Know by the light of faith that God is present, and be content with directing all your actions toward Him. Do all with a desire to please Him, irrespective of the consequences.

Useless thoughts spoil everything, and all mischief begins with useless thoughts. Reject them as soon as you perceive their presence in your mind, and return to communion with God.

In the beginning you may spend your appointed time of prayer simply rejecting wandering thoughts, and then falling back into thinking them. Some devotional methods may not work for you, but eventually you will develop a sweet time of fellowship with God.

The shortest way to go to God is not by mortifications of

your body, or other similar exercises that physically or mentally abuse your body or mind. Go straight to Him by a continual exercise of love and faith and doing all things for His sake.

Distinguish between an act of *understanding* and an act of the *will.* An act of the understanding is of very little value, but an act of the will is of utmost importance. Your supreme action must be loving and delighting yourself in God.

Dear Jesus, because I have been reading your Word, and because I have been studying the books of great Christian thinkers and leaders, my understanding of you and your will is growing by leaps and bounds. Keep me from mere intellectualism or a love of knowledge that never results in the moral transformation of my life. I seek true wisdom, which comes from the learned experiences of practicing the truth. Show me how every truth you reveal to me can be practiced, or show me the practical value of every Christian truth that I know. There is a beauty in truth that I could contemplate all day, but I seek to move beyond the contemplation of truth to the willing and doing of truth. I pray that your Holy Spirit would warn me of any dangers in my thought life, and I pray that your Spirit would motivate me and empower me to do the truth. May I truly live for you, as you fulfill your purposes in my life. Amen.

For the Lamb at the center of the throne will be their shepherd; he will lead them to springs of living water. They follow the Lamb wherever he goes. They were purchased from among men and offered as firstfruits to God and the Lamb.

Revelation 7:17; 14:4

6 Christ Glorified

"And surely I will be with you always." Who spoke these words? We must take time to know Him well if we are to understand what we may expect from Him as He offers to be with us all day long. Who is He? None other than the Lamb slain in the midst of the throne! The Lamb in His deepest humiliation is enthroned in the glory of God. He invites us to have the closest fellowship with Him, to become like Him.

It takes time, deep reverence, and adoring worship to come under the full impression that He who dwells in the glory of the Father, before whom all heaven bows in humble adoration, is none other than the One who offers to be my companion to lead me like a shepherd. Christ, dwelling in the glory of the Father, cares for every individual sheep in such a way as to make me one of those who follow the Lamb wherever He goes.

Read often the wonderful fifth chapter of Revelation until your heart is possessed by the one great thought of how all heaven falls prostrate and the elders cast their crowns before the throne. The Lamb reigns in the midst of the praises and the love of His ransomed people and the praises of all creation. The very Lamb of God comes to me in my daily life! He offers to walk with me and be my strength, my joy, and my almighty keeper. Surely I cannot expect Him to abide with me unless my heart bows before Him. If possible, I should be in a still deeper reverence by surrendering my life to His praise and service that I may be worthy of the love that has redeemed me.

Oh, Christian, believe that the Lamb in the midst of the throne is actually the embodiment of the omnipotent glory of the everlasting God and of His love. Believe that having the Lamb of God as your almighty shepherd and your faithful keeper does indeed make it possible for the thoughts and cares of earth not to prevail and separate you from His love for a single moment.

The Practice of the Presence of God

All possible kinds of bodily mortifications will not erase a single sin. You ought to expect, without any anxiety, the pardon of your sins through the shed blood of Jesus Christ, only endeavoring to love Him with all your heart. One of the notable monuments of His mercy is this: God seems to grant the greatest favors to the greatest sinners, who have come to Him through the blood of Christ.

The greatest pains or pleasures are not to be compared with what you can experience of them both when you are in a spiritual state. Do not worry about anything. Fear nothing. Desire only one thing from God: that you might not offend Him.

Thank God for all that you do, and acknowledge that all

your strength to do what is right comes from Him.

The foundation of the spiritual life is the high conception and esteem of God in faith. Faithfully reject any thought that would lower your esteem of God, and perform all of your actions for the love of God.

If you discover that you have not thought of God for a good while, acknowledge your wretchedness apart from Him. Then return to Him with a greater trust in Him, because you found yourself miserable through forgetting Him.

*D*ear Father God, thank you for sending your Son to die in my behalf; thank you for seating Him as the Lamb who was slain in the midst of your throne. Come now into my life, and set up your throne within my heart, guiding and directing my thoughts and decisions according to your perfect will. Lead me as a gentle shepherd, because I follow you willingly, asking only to be shown the way. When I am enjoying the greatest pleasures of life that you have provided, those pleasures are sweeter because you are with me sanctifying my delight in them. Help me to share the wonderful message of your forgiving and guiding love with others that they might know your saving grace and power. I pray that many will gather throughout the world to praise you and make your loving presence known. Amen.

Do you believe that I am able to do this?" "Yes, Lord," they replied.

Matthew 9:28

7
The Great Question

"Everything is possible for him who believes.' Immediately the boy's father exclaimed, 'I do believe; help me overcome my unbelief!' " (Mark 9:23, 24). "Jesus said to her [Martha], 'I am the resurrection and the life. He who believes in me will live, even though he dies; and whoever lives and believes in me will never die. Do you believe this?' 'Yes, Lord,' she told him, 'I believe that you are the Christ, the Son of God, who was to come into the world' " (John 11:25–27).

Because of what we have seen and heard of Jesus Christ, our hearts are ready to say with Martha, "I believe you are the Christ, the Son of God." However, when it comes to the point of believing what Christ promises us regarding the power of the resurrection life, of His abiding presence every day and all the day, we do not find it so easy to say, "I do believe that this omnipotent, omnipresent, unchangeable Christ, our Redeemer God, will actually walk with me all day, and give me the unceasing consciousness of His holy presence." It almost looks like too great a challenge to venture out with faith in His abiding presence. And yet, this is the faith that Christ asks us to have and *He* is waiting to work within us.

We must clearly understand the conditions by which Christ offers to reveal to us in experience the secret of His abiding presence. God cannot force His blessings on us against our will. He seeks in every possible way to stir up our desire, and to help us to realize that He is able and most willing to make His promises true. The resurrection of Christ from the dead is His great plea, His all-prevailing argument. If God could raise the dead Christ, who had died under the burden of all our sin and curse, surely He can (now that Christ has conquered death and is to us the Resurrection and the Life) fulfill in our hearts His promise that Christ can be so with us and in us in such a sense that He himself should be our life throughout the day.

And now, in view of what we have read and seen about Christ as our Lord, as our redeeming God, are we willing to take His word in all simplicity in its divine fullness of meaning and rest in the promise: "I will be with you all the day"? Christ's question comes to us: "Do you believe that I am able to do this?" Let us not rest until we have bowed before Him and said, "Yes, Lord, I do believe."

The Practice of the Presence of God

Trust in God and honor Him, and He will bestow great graces upon you.

God will never deceive you, and He will never let a person who is perfectly resigned to Him suffer long. Resolve: "I will endure everything for His sake."

You can learn to overcome the worry of anticipation. After

you begin to experience more and more the ready success of divine grace upon all occasions, you will not worry about things before they happen. When the time comes for you to do your duty, you will find God as in a clear mirror, and He will empower you and make you fit to fulfill your obligations.

Because of your many business affairs, sometimes you may find yourself diverted a little from the thought of God. After this happens, God will sometimes come to you with a fresh remembrance that will inflame and transport you in such a way that you may find it difficult to contain yourself.

When you become more aware of the presence of God in your life, you may find yourself more united in Him in your outward employments than when you leave them for times of devotion.

Dear God, it is far more easy for me to believe the content of the Scriptures than for me to believe that the promises you have made can really be effective in my life. Through much thought and study, I have come to believe that your Word is true, but I need more experiences of trusting you and your promises in specific situations to have my faith in your powerful presence in my life strengthened. Fill me with your Holy Spirit, remind me of your promises in the midst of my every need, strengthen my faith. Amen.

Whoever has my commands and obeys them, he is the one who loves me. He who loves me will be loved by my Father, and I too will love him and show [manifest, KJV] myself to him.

John 14:21

8
Christ Manifesting Himself

Christ promised the disciples that the Holy Spirit would come to reveal His presence as ever being with them. When the Spirit came, He through the Spirit would manifest himself to them. They would know Him in a new, divine, spiritual way. In the power of the Spirit they would know Him and have Him far more intimately and unceasingly with them than they ever had upon earth.

The condition of this revelation of himself is comprised in the one word—love: "Whoever has my commands and obeys them, he is the one who loves me. He who loves me will be loved by my Father, and I too will love him and show myself to him." God intends for a meeting of divine and human love. The love with which Christ had loved the disciples had taken possession of their hearts, and would show itself in their love with a full and absolute obedience. The Father would see this, and His love would rest upon them. Christ would love them with the special love drawn out by the loving heart and would manifest himself to them. The love of heaven shed abroad in their hearts would be met by the new and blessed revelation of Christ himself.

But this is not all. When the question was asked, "But Lord, why do you intend to show yourself to us and not to the world?" Jesus replied with a repetition of the words, "If anyone loves me, he will obey my teaching. My Father will love him, and we will come to him and make our home with him" (John 14:23). In the heart prepared by the Holy Spirit, which shows itself in the obedience of love in a fully surrendered heart, the Father and the Son will take up their home.

Now, Christ promises nothing less than this: "And surely I will be with you always." The "with" implies "in." Christ with the Father will dwell in the heart by faith. Oh, if everyone would enter into the secret of the abiding presence, if they would only study, believe, and claim in childlike simplicity the blessed promise: "I will show myself to him."

The Practice of the Presence of God

You may have some great pain of body or mind, but the worst that can happen to you is the loss of the sense of God you have come to enjoy. However, the goodness of God assures us that He will not utterly forsake us. He will give you the strength to bear whatever evil He permits to happen to you; therefore, fear nothing.

Sometimes after consulting someone about your troubles, you may find yourself even more perplexed. When you become conscious of your readiness to lay down your life for God, you may lose your apprehension of danger. Perfect resignation to God is a sure way to heaven, a way in which you will always have sufficient light for your conduct.

In the beginning of your spiritual life, you ought to be faithful in doing your duty and denying yourself. After that, unspeakable pleasures will follow.

In every difficulty, you need only go to Jesus Christ, ask Him for His grace, and things will become easy.

Many do not advance in Christian progress because they stick in penances and particular devotional exercises while they neglect the love of God, which is the *end*, purpose, or reason for the Christian life. To go to God, you only need a heart resolutely determined to apply itself supremely to Him, or for *His* sake, and to love Him only.

*D*ear Jesus, thank you for keeping the Christian faith so absolutely simple and yet so profound that the so-called wisdom of this world cannot comprehend it. You gave your Word to work a moral transformation in the lives of your people. As I obey you from a heart full of love, you have promised to be with me in a way that I can certainly know. I pray that your Holy Spirit will begin to apply the truth of your Word to the hearts and minds of people in a new and more powerful way. I pray that your Holy Spirit will use the truth of your Word to convict sinners of their sin, lead them to repentance, and empower them to daily obedience. May we always tell others of your loving grace. Amen.

Jesus said to her, "Mary." She turned toward him and cried out in Aramaic, "Rabboni!" (which means Teacher).

John 20:16

9

Mary: The Morning Watch

Here we have the first manifestation of the risen Savior when He appeared to Mary Magdalene, the woman who loved much.

Think of what the morning watch meant to Mary. The morning watch proves an intense longing of love that will not rest until it has found the Lord it seeks. In her longing to find Christ, she separated herself from all else, even from the chief of the apostles. She struggled against fear with a faith that refused to let go until it received His wonderful promise. Her morning watch resulted in Christ's coming and fulfilling the promise: "If anyone loves me, he will obey my teaching. My Father will love him, and we will come to him and make our home with him" (John 14:23). Her love was met by the love of Jesus, and she found Him, the living Lord, in all the power of His resurrection life. She now understood what He had said about ascending to the Father, to the life of divine and omnipotent glory. In her morning watch, she received the commission from her Lord to go and tell His brethren of what she had heard from Him.

That first morning watch, waiting for the risen Lord to reveal himself, is a prophecy and a pledge of what the morning watch has been to thousands of people! In fear and doubt, and yet with a burning love and strong hope, they have waited for Him. Then He, of whom they had known very little because of their feeble human apprehension, has breathed upon them in the power of His resurrection life, manifesting himself as the Lord of Glory. There they have learned (not in words or thought but in the reality of a divine experience) what it means to be taken up into the keeping of His abiding presence, into the presence of the One to whom all power has been given on earth and in heaven.

And what are we to learn? That nothing can prove a greater attraction to our Lord than the love that sacrifices everything and rests satisfied with nothing less than knowing Him and His abiding presence. To this type of love Christ will manifest himself. He loved us and gave himself for us. Christ wants our love so He can reveal His love. To our love He speaks the word: "And surely I will be with you always." True love accepts, rejoices in, and lives in His Word.

The Practice of the Presence of God

If you want to accustom yourself to a continual conversation with Christ, with freedom and simplicity, you must begin *in one hearty renunciation* of everything which you know does not lead to God.

You only need to recognize God intimately present with

you to address yourself to Him every moment. You may ask for His assistance in knowing His will in things that are doubtful, and for rightly performing those duties which you plainly see He requires of you. God always gives us light in our doubts when we have no other design but to please Him. Offer to Him everything you do, and thank Him for everything you have done when completed.

In your conversation with God, praise Him, adore Him, and love Him without ceasing because of His infinite goodness and perfection.

Do not be discouraged on account of your sins, but pray for His grace with a perfect confidence in our Lord Jesus Christ. God never fails to offer you His grace in every action, and you will distinctly perceive it unless your thoughts have wandered from a sense of God's presence or you have forgotten to ask for His assistance.

Your sanctification does not depend upon changing your works, but in doing for God's sake what you commonly do for your own. Do not confuse the means with the end! Do not become addicted to "works" performed with selfish regard.

*D*ear Jesus, thank you for talking to Mary in the morning watch. I know that you did because the Bible is true. But, Lord, strengthen my faith in you and in the everyday application of your Word, so that I may be encouraged to come seeking you in the morning watch, and through seeking you in love with a desire to obey, find you. Amen.

But they urged him strongly, "Stay [abide, KJV] with us, for it is nearly evening; the day is almost over." So he went in to stay with them. Then their eyes were opened . . .

Luke 24:29,31

10
Emmaus: The Evening Prayer

If Mary teaches us what the morning watch can be for the revelation of Jesus to our souls, Emmaus reminds us of the place the evening prayer may have in preparing us for the full manifestation of Christ to us.

The two disciples began the day in thick darkness. When at length the women told of the angel who had said that Jesus was alive, they knew not what to think. When He himself drew near, they did not recognize Him, and they knew Him not. Jesus often comes near us with the one object of manifesting himself, but He is hindered because we are so slow of heart to believe what the Word has spoken. But as the Lord spoke with them, their hearts began to burn within, and yet there never was a thought that it might be Jesus. It is often that way now. The Word becomes precious to us in the fellowship of the saints; our hearts are stirred with the new vision of what Christ's presence may be, and yet—we see Him not.

When the Lord seemed as though to go on farther,

their prayer, "Abide with us," constrained Him. In that night, Christ gave a new meaning to the word "abide." They did not yet understand it, but in the use of the word they received far more than they expected—a foretaste of the life of abiding that the resurrection had now made possible. Let us learn the lesson of how much we need, toward the close of the day, to pause, perhaps in fellowship with others, and with the whole heart take up anew the promise of the abiding presence, and pray with the urgency that constrains us: "Abide, abide with us."

Now what is the chief lesson of the story? What led our Lord to reveal himself to these two men? Nothing less than this: their intense devotion to their Lord. There may be much ignorance and unbelief, but if there is a burning desire that above everything longs for Him, a desire that is ever fostered as the Word is heard or spoken, we may count upon it: He will make himself known to us. To such intense devotion and constraining prayer, the Lord's message will be given in power: "And surely I will be with you always." Our eyes will be opened, and we will know Him and the blessed secret of the abiding presence always. It is to strong desire and constraining prayer that Christ will most assuredly manifest himself.

The Practice of the Presence of God

The most excellent method for going to God is to do your common business without any view of pleasing others, and, as far as you are capable, purely for the love of God.

You are as strictly obligated to adhere to God by action in your times of action as you are by prayer in your times of prayer.

Sometimes in prayer you will experience only a sense of the presence of God, your soul being insensible to everything except His divine love in your heart. When your appointed time for prayer is over, you may sense no difference because you will still continue with God, praising and blessing Him with all your might, so that your life is one of continual joy.

Remember: "You must once and for all heartily put your whole trust in God, secure that He will never deceive you, and make a total surrender of yourself to Him."

Never grow weary of doing little things for the love of God, who does not regard the greatness of the work but the love with which it is performed. In the beginning you may fail in your endeavors, but you will gain a habit of allowing love to act through you to your exceeding delight.

*D*ear Father, I thank you for the times of rest as well as for the times of work. In the morning I can rise and cast my first thoughts upon you, and in the evening before I close my eyes in sleep, I can praise you and cast my cares into your hands. Waking and sleeping, you are present with me; teach me even in my dreams for the sake of Jesus. Amen.

On the evening of that first day of the week, when the disciples were together, with the doors locked for fear of the Jews, Jesus came and stood among them and said, "Peace be with you."

John 20:19

11
The Disciples: Their Divine Mission

The disciples received the message of Mary. Peter told them that he had seen the Lord. Later in the evening, the men from Emmaus saw Jesus. Through these appearances, the disciples were prepared for what came next, when Jesus stood in their midst and said, "Peace be with you," and showed them His hands and feet. This was not only to be a sign of recognition, but the deep eternal mystery of what would be seen in heaven when He was in the midst of the throne, "a Lamb as it had been slain."

The Apostle wrote about His appearance, saying, "The disciples were overjoyed when they saw the Lord" (John 20:20). And Jesus said to them, "Peace be with you! As the Father has sent me, I am sending you" (John 20:21). To Mary, Jesus revealed himself to the fervent love that could not rest without Him. The men at Emmaus received the revelation because of their constraining prayer. Here He met with the willing servants whom He had trained for His service, and handed over to them the work He had done on earth. He changed their fear into the boldness of peace and gladness. He ascended to the Father; the work the Father had given Him to do He now entrusted to them to make known and carry on to victory.

For their divine work they needed divine power. So, He breathed upon them the resurrection life He had won by His death. He fulfilled His promise: "I live, and you shall live also." The exceeding greatness of the mighty power of God by which He raised Christ from the dead, none other than the Spirit of holiness by which He, as the Son of God, was raised from the dead, will henceforth work in them. All that was bound or loosed in that power would be bound or loosed in heaven.

The story comes to us with wonderful power. To us the word is also spoken: "As the Father sent me, so I am sending you." For us, too, the personal manifestation of Jesus is of the living One with the pierced hands and feet. If our hearts are set on nothing less than the presence of the living Lord, we may be confident it will be given us. Jesus never sends His servants out without the promise of His abiding presence and His almighty power.

The Practice of the Presence of God

The whole substance of Christianity is faith, hope, and love, by the practice of which we become united to the will of God. All things are possible to the person who *believes*. They are less difficult to the person who *hopes*. They are more easy to the person who *loves*; and still more easy to the person who perseveres in the practice of these three virtues.

The end that you should propose for yourself in this life is to be the most perfect worshiper of God you can possibly be, and as you hope to be through all eternity.

When you enter upon the spiritual life, you should consider and examine to the bottom what you are. You should discover that you do not deserve the name "Christian." You should discover that you are fallen, and that God will humble you by many pains and labors. After this, you should not wonder that troubles, temptations, oppositions, and contradictions will happen to you from others. Bear with them, as long as God pleases, as things to your advantage.

The greater the perfection you aspire after, the more dependent you will be upon divine grace.

Consider God as the goal of all your thoughts and desires, as the mark to which they should tend and in which they should end. Spend your times of private prayer thinking of God and submitting yourself to the truths of faith, so as to convince your mind of, and to impress deeply upon your heart, His divine existence. By this method you will increase in the knowledge and love of God. Resolve to live in a continual sense of His presence.

Dear Jesus, you prepared the hearts of the disciples before you presented yourself to them in your resurrection glory. I submit myself wholeheartedly to you, and ask you to guide my devotions and all my thoughts. Prepare me to know more of your presence in my life each day. Amen.

Then Jesus told him,
"Because you have seen me,
you have believed; blessed
are those who have not seen
and yet have believed."

John 20:29

12
Thomas: The Blessedness of Believing

We all count the blessedness of Thomas as something very wonderful: Christ manifesting himself and allowing Thomas to touch His hands and His side. No wonder that this blessedness can find no words but those of holy adoration: "My Lord and my God." Has there ever been a higher expression of the overwhelming nearness of the glory of God?

And yet Christ said, "Because you have seen me, you have believed; blessed are those who have not seen and yet have believed" (John 20:29). True and living faith gives a sense of Christ's divine nearness far deeper and more intimate than even the joy that filled the heart of Thomas. Here, even now, after the lapse of all these centuries, we may experience the presence and power of Christ in a far deeper reality than Thomas did. To those who see not, yet believe—simply, only, truly, fully believe in what Christ is and can be to them every moment—He has promised that He will manifest himself, and that the Father and He will come and dwell in them.

Have we not often been inclined to think of this full life of faith as something beyond our reach? Such a thought robs us of the power to believe. Let us take hold of Christ's word: "Blessed are those who have not seen and yet believe." Indeed, the heavenly blessing which fills the whole heart and life receives the love and the presence of the living Lord through faith.

You ask how to come to this childlike faith. The answer is very simple. When Jesus Christ is the one object of your desire and your confidence, He will manifest himself in divine power. Thomas had proved his intense devotion to Christ when he said, "Let us go, that we may die with Him." To such a love, even when it is struggling with unbelief, Jesus Christ will manifest himself. He will make His holy promise an actual reality in your conscious experience: "And surely I will be with you always." Let us see to it that our faith in His blessed Word, in His divine power, in His holy abiding presence, masters our whole being, and Christ will actually manifest himself, abide with us, and dwell in our hearts as His home.

The Practice of the Presence of God

Consider what you have to do to complete your business, when and how each thing should be done, and then spend the intervals of your time, as well as before and after work, in prayer. When in prayer, fill your mind with great thoughts of the infinite God.

Before you begin your business, pray as I have: "Thou art with me, and I must now, in obedience to Thy commands, apply my mind to these outward things. I beseech Thee to grant me the grace to continue in Thy presence; and to this end do Thou prosper me with Thy assistance, receive all my works, and possess all my affections."

As you do your work, continue as you can your familiar conversation with your Maker, implore His grace, and offer Him all your actions.

When you have done your duty, examine yourself to see how you did. If well, give thanks to God. If otherwise, ask for His pardon, and without being discouraged set your mind right again and continue to be in the presence of God as if you had never faltered. By rising from your falls in this way, by renewing acts of faith and love, you will come to a state of thankfulness before God.

Your example of walking in the presence of God will be a stronger inducement to others to do likewise than any arguments you can propose. Pray that your very countenance of a sweet and calm devotion will edify others. Even in the greatest hurry of business, you can preserve your recollection of God and your heavenly mindedness. You can work with an even, uninterrupted composure and tranquillity of spirit. The time of business should not make you different from the type of person you are in prayer.

*D*ear Lord Jesus, thank you for blessed times of quiet and peaceful times of prayer. Thank you for filling my heart with your love. Please be with me and transform me in such a way that I do not deviate in the pressures of work from the type of person I try to be in times of prayer. Amen.

The third time he said to him, "Simon son of John, do you love me?" Peter was hurt because Jesus asked him the third time, "Do you love me?" He said, "Lord, you know all things; you know that I love you." Jesus said, "Feed my sheep."

John 21:17

13

Peter: The Greatness of Love

After His resurrection, Christ first revealed himself to Mary, to the one who loved much. Then Peter had his first vision of the Lord. Next, He made himself known in the supper at Emmaus. Then He appeared to the ten, and later revealed himself to Thomas. Christ always manifested himself to the intense devotion of the prepared heart. And now in this manifestation of himself to Peter, love is again the keynote.

We can easily understand why Christ asked the question three times, "Do you love me?" He needed to remind Peter of the terrible self-confidence in which he had said, "Even if I have to die with you, I will never disown you" (Matt. 26:35). Peter needed a quiet, deep heart-searching before he could be sure that his love was real and true. Peter needed a deep penitence and a consciousness of how little he could trust himself. Love was the one thing he needed to have a full restoration of his place in the heart of Jesus. Love was the first and highest condition for him to feed His sheep and care for His lambs.

God is love. Christ is the Son of His love. Having loved His own, He loved them to the uttermost, and said, "As the Father loved me, so love I you." He asked them to prove their love to Him by keeping His commandments and loving each other with the love with which He loved them. In heaven and on earth, in the Father and in the Son, in us, in all our work for Him and in our care for souls, the greatest thing is love.

To everyone who longs to have Jesus manifest himself to them, the chief, the essential requisite is love. Peter teaches us that such love is not in the power of men to offer. Such love came to him through the power of Christ's death to sin and the power of His resurrection life, of which Peter became partaker. As he puts it in his first epistle: "Though you have not seen him, you love him; and even though you do not see him now, you believe in him and are filled with an inexpressible and glorious joy" (1 Pet. 1:8). Thank God, if Peter the self-confident could be so changed, can we not believe that Christ will work in us the wondrous change, too, manifesting himself to a loving heart in all the fullness of His precious word: "And surely I am with you always"! Christ will manifest himself to love, and only love will make you fit for feeding His sheep and tending His lambs.

The Practice of the Presence of God

Give yourself wholly to God that He might take away your sin. Renounce, for the love of Him, everything that is not of Him, and begin to live as though God were the most important person in the world.

Sometimes you may need to consider yourself before Him as a poor criminal at the feet of his judge; at other times you will behold Him in your heart as a Father, as your God. Worship God as often as you can. Keep your mind in His holy presence, and recall Him as often as your mind wanders from Him.

Make the worship of God and prayer to God as much your business all day long as at your appointed times of prayer and worship. You must have periods of time when you can drive away from your mind everything that is capable of interrupting your thoughts of God. Even in the heights of some labors, you can be conscious of praising God.

Consider any advancement you make in your spiritual life due to the mere mercy and goodness of God, because you can do nothing apart from Him.

Be faithful to keep yourself in His holy presence, and set Him always before you; this will hinder your offending Him and doing anything willfully to displease Him.

*D*ear Lord Jesus, I am conscious that I love you, but so was Peter before he denied you. I cannot love with a steadfast, dependable love unless you indwell me and love through me. Make your loving presence known to others through me. Make me the type of person you wanted Peter to become when you told him to feed your sheep. Amen.

When I saw him, I fell at his feet as though dead. Then he placed his right hand on me and said: "Do not be afraid. I am the First and the Last. I am the Living One; I was dead, and behold I am alive for ever and ever!"

Revelation 1:17, 18

14
John: Life From the Dead

Here we have Christ manifesting himself to the beloved disciple sixty or more years after the resurrection. John fell as though dead at His feet. God had said to Moses, in answer to his prayer "Show me your glory": "You cannot see my face, for no one may see me and live" (Ex. 33:18). Because men are sinners, they cannot receive the vision of the divine glory and live. We need the death of Christ to open the way for the life of God in glory to enter in. When John fell as though dead at Christ's feet, it proved how little he could endure the wonderful heavenly vision.

Christ laid His right hand upon him and said, "Do not be afraid. I am the Living One; I was dead, and behold I am alive for ever and ever!" He reminded him that He, too, had passed through death before He could rise to the life and the glory of God. For the Master himself and for every disciple, for Moses and for John, there is only one way to the glory of God—death to all that has been in contact with sin.

The lesson is a deep and most needed one for all who long for Jesus to manifest himself to them. The knowledge of Jesus, fellowship with Him and the experience of His power, is not possible without the sacrifice of all there is in us of the world and its spirit. The disciples experienced this from Christ's first ordination charge (reported in Matt. 10:37–39). He spoke about forsaking father and mother, about taking up the cross, about losing our life for His sake; down to the days before His death when He said, "I tell you the truth, unless a kernel of wheat falls to the ground and dies, it remains only a single seed. But if it dies, it produces many seeds. The man who loves his life will lose it, while the man who hates his life in this world will keep it for eternal life" (John 12:24, 25). Christ made this the one great charge: Deny self; bear the cross, and follow me.

We are seeking to find out the secret of getting into touch with the Lord Jesus Christ so His abiding presence shall be our portion every day. Let us accept the lesson: through death to life. In the power of Christ Jesus (with whom we have been crucified, and whose death now works in us, if we will yield ourselves to it), death to sin and to the world with all its self-pleasing and self-exaltation must be the deepest law of our spiritual life. Peter said to Christ, "Spare thyself" (marginal note, Matt. 16:22, KJV). Jesus said to him, "Deny yourself." The disciples followed Christ even to the cross; therefore, they were prepared to receive their Master's word: "And surely I will be with you always."

The Practice of the Presence of God

Keep yourself in the presence of God and you will have a holy freedom and a familiarity with God that will allow you to ask successfully for the graces you need daily.

By repeating acts of prayer and devotion, they will become habits, and the presence of God will become natural to you.

Thank God for all His goodness toward you. Thank Him for His many favors. May all things praise Him!

Give yourself up to God as the best return you can make for His love to you. And for love of Him, renounce all besides Him.

You will find great delight and consolation when you apply your mind carefully, even in the midst of your business, to the presence of God. Always consider Him as *with* you as well as *in* you. Practicing His presence will produce so high an esteem for God that only *faith*, apart from works of the law or devotional methods, will satisfy you as the way to God.

Dear Father, thank you for the marvelous revelation of your Son to John as reported in the book of Revelation. What a picture of the Lamb upon the throne! What a scene of divine love and grace! Send your Holy Spirit to me, and grant me a deeper knowledge of Christ than I have ever known. Amen.

But when God, who set me apart from birth and called me by his grace, was pleased to reveal his Son in me so that I might preach him among the Gentiles, I did not consult any man.

Galatians 1:15, 16

15
Paul: Christ Revealed in Him

In all our study and worship of Christ, we find our thoughts ever gathering around these five points: The incarnate Christ, the crucified Christ, the enthroned Christ, the indwelling Christ, and the Christ coming in glory. If the first be the seed, the second is the seed cast into the ground, and the third the seed growing up to the very heaven. Then follows the fruit through the Holy Spirit, Christ dwelling in the heart; and then the gathering of the fruit into the storehouse when Christ appears.

Paul tells us that it pleased God to reveal His Son in him. And he gives his testimony to the result of that revelation: "Christ lives in me" (Gal. 2:20). Of his life he says that the chief mark is that he is crucified with Christ. This enables him to say, "I no longer live"; in Christ he had found the death of self. Just as the cross is the chief characteristic of Christ himself: "A Lamb, looking as if it had been slain standing in the center of the throne," so the life of Christ in Paul made him inseparably one with his crucified Lord. So completely was this the case that he could say, "May I never boast except in the cross of our Lord Jesus Christ, through which the world has been crucified to me, and I to the world" (Gal. 6:14).

If you could ask Paul, "If Christ so actually lives in you that you no longer live, what becomes of your responsibility?", the answer would be ready and clear: "I live by faith in the Son of God, who loved me and gave himself for me" (Gal. 2:20). His life was every moment a life of faith in Him who had loved him and given himself so completely that He had undertaken at all times to be the life of His willing disciple.

This was the sum and substance of all Paul's preaching. He asks for intercession that he might speak "the mystery of God, namely, Christ"; to "them God has chosen to make known among the Gentiles the glorious riches of this mystery, which is Christ in you, the hope of glory" (Col. 2:2; 1:27). The indwelling Christ was the secret of his life of faith, the one power, the one aim of all his life and work, the hope of glory. Let us believe in the abiding presence of Christ as the sure gift to each one who trusts Him fully.

The Practice of the Presence of God

Early in your devotional life, it may seem that all creatures, reason, and God himself are against you. You may suffer from the apprehension that you are not devoted to God as you wish to be and your past sins are always before your mind. Recognition of the great unmerited favors of God to you may also be a source of suffering. These things will convince you that you can come before God on the basis of faith alone.

Your troubles should not diminish the trust you have in God, but can serve to increase your faith. Then, your soul which seemed so troubled before may come to feel a profound inward peace, centered in God and at rest.

Eventually, you will be able to walk before God simply, in faith, with humility and love, applying yourself diligently to doing nothing and thinking nothing which may displease Him.

Hope that when you have done what you can, He will do with you what He pleases.

You will have no difficulty about your spiritual state when you have no will but that of God's will, which you endeavor to accomplish and to which you are so resigned that you would not even take up a straw from the ground against His order, or from any other motive than pure love to Him.

*D*ear Father, thank you for revealing the great mystery of the gospel to the faithful apostles of Jesus Christ, who spread the good news of Christ living in us to others. I pray that through faith His presence in me and with me will become more real to me in experience. I do not ask this for selfish reasons, but I desire the presence of Christ with me in power so I can go and tell others of the wonderful mystery you want them to enjoy for Christ's sake. Amen.

Then the disciples came to Jesus in private and asked, "Why couldn't we drive it out?" He replied, "Because you have so little faith. . . . This kind does not go out except by prayer and fasting."

Matthew 17:19–21

16
Why Could We Not?

The disciples had often cast out demons. But here they had been impotent. They asked the Lord what the reason might be. His answer is very simple: "Because of your little faith."

We have here the reply to the great question so often asked. How is it that we cannot live that life of unbroken fellowship with Christ which the Scriptures promise? Simply because of our unbelief. We do not realize that faith must accept and expect that God will, by His almighty power, fulfill every promise He has made. We do not live in that utter helplessness and dependence on God alone which is the very essence of faith. We are not strong in the faith, fully persuaded that what God has promised He is able and willing to perform. We do not give ourselves with our whole heart simply to believe that God by His almighty power will work wonders in our hearts.

What can be the reason that this faith is so often lacking? Why does this kind not go out except by prayer and fasting? To have a strong faith in God demands a life in close touch with Him by persistent prayer. We cannot call up faith at our bidding; it requires close fellowship with God. It requires not only prayer but fasting, too, in the larger and deeper meaning of that word. It requires the denial of self, the sacrifice of that pleasing of the flesh and the eye and the pride of life, which is the essence of a worldly spirit. To gain the prizes of the heavenly life here on earth calls for the sacrifice of all that earth can offer. Just as it takes God to satisfy the human heart and work His mighty miracles in it, it takes the whole man utterly given up to God to have the power of that faith which can cast out every evil spirit. "Prayer and fasting" is essential.

The Practice of the Presence of God

Make it your business only to persevere in His holy presence, wherein you keep yourself by simple attention and a general fond regard to God. I call this an *actual presence* of God.

To keep yourself in the actual presence of God, remain in habitual, silent, and secret conversation with God, which will cause you joys and raptures inwardly, and sometimes outwardly. Sometimes you may be forced to moderate your inward joys to prevent their appearance to others.

When you find yourself full of sinful corruptions, and realize that you have committed all sorts of crimes against your God and King, touched with a sense of regret, confess to Him all your wickedness and ask for His forgiveness. Abandon yourself to His hands that He may do what pleases Him, and you will find your King full of mercy and goodness. Far from chastising you, He will embrace you with love, make you eat at His table, serve you with

His own hands, and give you the key to His treasures.

Through practicing the actual presence with Him, He will converse and delight himself incessantly with you in a thousand different ways, and treat you in all respects as His favorite person.

My most useful method is this simple attention, and such a general passionate regard to God, to whom I find myself often attached with greater sweetness and delight than that of an infant at the mother's breast; so that, if I dare use the expression, I should choose to call this state the bosom of God—for the inexpressible sweetness which I taste and experience there.

*D*ear heavenly Father, what is fasting and prayer if not times of total and uninterrupted practice of your holy presence? Indeed, I can find myself so wrapped up in religious duties or social concerns that I forget to eat—a form of fasting. But I pray that you would be so present with me that I would lose track of time in my prayers, not notice any hunger, but experience only the inexpressible joy of your presence. And yet, I will set aside times to pray and fast, because I want to be in such a close relationship with you that you can use me to save others. Amen.

The one who sent me is with me; he has not left me alone, for I always do what pleases him.

John 8:29

17 The Power of Obedience

In these words Christ not only tells what His life with the Father was, but reveals at the same time the law of all fellowship with God: simple obedience.

How strongly He insisted upon it in the farewell discourse. In chapter 14 He says three times, "Whoever has my commands and *obeys* them, he is the one who loves me. He who loves me will be loved by my Father, and I too will love him and show myself to him. . . . My Father will love him, and we will come to him and make our home with him" (John 14:21, 23). And also three times over in chapter 15: "If you remain in me and my words remain in you, ask whatever you wish, and it will be given you"; "If you obey my commands, you will remain in my love, just as I have obeyed my Father's command and remain in his love"; "You are my friends if you do what I command" (John 15:7, 10, 14).

Obedience proves your love for God and demonstrates that His love has been shed abroad in your heart by the

Holy Spirit. Obedience comes from love and leads to love, a deeper and a fuller experience of God's love and indwelling. Obedience assures us what we ask will be given us. It assures us we are abiding in the love of Christ. It seals our claim to be called the friends of Christ. Obedience is not only a proof of love but also of faith, assuring us "whatsoever we ask, we receive of him because we keep his commandments, and do the things that are pleasing in his sight" (1 John 3:22, KJV).

For the abiding enjoyment of His holy presence, simple, full obedience is necessary. The new covenant has made full provision for this: "I will put my law in their minds and write it on their hearts. I will be their God, and they will be my people" (Jer. 31:33). "I will give you a new heart and put a new spirit in you; I will remove from you your heart of stone and give you a heart of flesh. And I will put my Spirit in you and move you to follow my decrees and be careful to keep my laws" (Ezek. 36:26, 27).

Blessed obedience enables us to abide in His love and gives the full experience of His unbroken presence. Christ did not speak of an impossibility; He saw what in the power of the Spirit we might confidently expect. Let the thought take deep hold of us: it is to the obedient that the word comes, "And surely I will be with you always," and to whom all the fullness of its meaning will be revealed.

The Practice of the Presence of God

Sometimes by necessity or infirmity, your thoughts may wander from practicing the presence of God. But presently, His Holy Spirit will recall you by inward motions so charming and delicious that you will be too amazed to mention them.

Set hours of prayer will become for you only a continuation of the same practice of the presence. Sometimes you may desire to present yourself to God as a stone before a carver, desiring Him to form His perfect image in your soul and make you entirely as himself.

At other times, when you apply yourself to prayer, you will feel your spirit and soul being lifted up without any concern or effort of your own. You will continue in prayer as though suspended and firmly fixed in God as your center and place of rest.

Practicing the presence of God is not inactivity, delusion, or self-love, as some may charge. It is a holy inactivity, but in this state the soul is incapable of self-love, even though it would be a happy self-love. Because the soul which enjoys God in this way desires nothing but Him, the practice of the presence should not be called delusion.

Let God do what He pleases with you. Desire only Him, to be wholly devoted to Him.

*D*ear God, your Word has made what you require of us so perfectly clear: you desire a clean heart and loving obedience. Purify my heart by removing all iniquity from my life by the power of your Holy Spirit. I desire to be wholly transformed by your indwelling presence. I want to be with you every moment, and ask that you would give me the happy satisfaction of being used by you. Amen.

We will give our attention to prayer. The church was earnestly praying to God for him.

Acts 6:4; 12:5

18
The Power of Intercession

We must pray for and believe in the unlimited power of united intercession. Missionaries who have been in the field and who have penetrated most deeply into the heart of the problem press upon Christians the *imperative need of more intercession—above all, of united intercession.*

"We can in no way better serve the deepest interest of the churches than by multiplying the number of real intercessors, and by focusing the prayers of Christians upon those great situations which demand the almighty working of the Spirit of God. Far more important and vital than any service we can render to missions is that of helping to release the superhuman energy of prayer, and through uniting in this holy ministry true intercessors of all lands, to help the ushering in of a new era abounding in signs and wonders characteristic of the working of the living Christ. Immeasurably more important than any other work is the linking of all we do to the fountain of divine life and energy. The Christian world has not only a right to expect mission leaders to set forth the facts and methods of the work, but also a larger discovery of superhuman resources and a greater irradiation of spiritual power."[1]

And where is there a greater need of focusing the united intercession of Christians than on the great army of missionaries? They confess the need of the presence and the power of God's Spirit in their life and work. They long for the experience of the abiding presence and power of Christ every day. They need it. They have a right to it. Shall we not, those of us desiring the secret of the presence, form a part of that great army that pleads with God for the enduement of power which is so absolutely necessary for effective work? Shall we not, like the early apostles, "give our attention to prayer" until God sends an abundant answer? As we give ourselves continually to prayer, the power of the promise, "And surely I will be with you always," will be proved in our lives.

The Practice of the Presence of God

We have a God who is infinitely gracious and knows all our needs. He will come in His own time, and when you least expect it. Hope in Him more than ever. Thank Him for the favors He does for you, particularly for the fortitude and patience which He gives you in your afflictions. They are a plain mark of His care for you. Comfort yourself with Him, and give thanks for all.

The Spirit can give you a good disposition and a good will.

[1]The quote is from John R. Mott (1865–1955), an ecumenical missions leader that Andrew Murray (1828–1917) would have heard of early in Mott's career.

Affliction which God sends can prove a wholesome remedy to your character defects, and encourage you to put all your trust in God who goes with you everywhere.

Think of God as often as you can, especially in the greatest dangers. Lifting your heart to Him will suffice. A little remembering of God, one act of inward worship, though in the midst of battle, your prayers, however short, are very acceptable to God. Such prayers will fortify a soldier's courage in occasions of danger.

Thank God for everything as completely as you can. Repeat often in the day the small but holy exercises of internal adorations.

Think of God as often as you can, especially if you are a soldier who is daily exposed to the dangers of life. God will assist you and your entire family.

*D*ear God, thank you for calling me to be a soldier in the army of your Son, Jesus Christ. Thank you for calling me to do battle against the principalities and powers that seek to destroy your kingdom and people everywhere. Thank you for calling me to pray on behalf of missionaries around the world. Thank you for promising that my prayers in their behalf will make a difference in the spiritual battlefield. But help me to love my enemies as I do battle, so I might further the eventual triumph of your love. Amen.

My times are in your hands.

Psalms 31:15

19 The Power of Time

The plural implies the singular: My time is in your hands. It belongs to you. You alone have a right to command it. I yield it wholly and gladly to your disposal. What mighty power time can exert if wholly given up to God!

Time is lord of all things. What is all the history of the world but a proof of how, slowly but surely, time has made man what he is today? All around us we see the proofs. In the growth of the child to manhood, both physically and mentally, in the success of every pursuit, in all our labors and all our attainments, it is under the law of time and its inconceivable power that we spend our lives.

This is especially true in religion and fellowship with God. Here time is also master. What fellowship with God! What holiness and blessedness! What likeness to His image, and what power in His service for blessing to men! All on the one condition: that we have sufficient time with God for His holiness to shine on us with its light and its heat, and to make us partakers of His Spirit and His life. The very essence of religion lies in the thought: Time with God.

And yet how many of God's servants there are who, while giving their lives to His service, frankly confess that the feebleness of their spiritual life, and the inadequate results of their Christian service as a whole, are due to the failure to set aside time, and to use it rightly, for daily communion with God.

What can be the cause at the back of this sad confession? Nothing but a lack of faith in the God-given assurance that time spent alone with God will indeed bring into the life of His servants the power to enable them so to use all their times in His fellowship that His abiding presence will be with them all the day.

Oh, you who are complaining that overwork, or too much zeal in doing the work, is hindering your spiritual efficiency, do you not see that if you would but submit your timetable to the inspection of Christ and His Holy Spirit, you would find that a new life would be yours if you fully believed and put into daily practice the word: My time is in thy hand?

The Practice of the Presence of God

Make it your aim to be always with God, and to do nothing, say nothing, and think nothing that may displease Him. Do this without any other view than purely for your love of God and because He deserves infinitely more.

You may become so accustomed to the divine presence that you will knowingly receive from God continual assistance upon all occasions, and be filled with joys so continual and sometimes so great that you may be forced to use means to moderate them and to hinder their outward appearance.

If you are sometimes too much absent from the divine presence, God will at this point urge your soul to recall Him. This may happen often while you are engaged in outward business.

When God moves within your soul, answer with faith and loyalty to His inward drawings, either by the elevation of your heart toward God, by a meek and fond regard to Him, or by those words love may form upon your lips, such as, "My God, here I am, all devoted to you. Lord, make me according to your heart."

Sometimes you may feel God so satisfied with your words of praise and love that He will give you a sense of His peace and loving rest in the center of your soul. These experiences will give you such an assurance that God is always in the reservoir and bottom of your soul that you will be incapable of doubting it.

Dear God, you have not called me to pattern my life after any other human being, even though that person may have been greatly used by you or had wonderful spiritual encounters with you. You have called me, however, to imitate your Son, Jesus Christ. Your apostles have told us to imitate them, but only as they have imitated our Lord Jesus Christ. Help me to model the spirit and attitude of your Son to others in all situations. Encourage me to spend the necessary time with you so you can transform my life to be such a witness. Lift me when I fall, and help me to know your presence in my life always for Jesus' sake. Amen.

Everything is possible for him who believes.

Mark 9:23

20
The Power of Faith

Scripture teaches us that there is not one truth on which Christ insisted more frequently, both with His disciples and with those who came seeking His help, than the absolute necessity of faith and its unlimited possibilities. Experience has taught us that there is nothing in which we come so short as the simple and absolute trust in God to fulfill literally in us all that He has promised. A life in the abiding presence must of necessity be a life of unceasing faith.

Think for a moment of the marks of true faith. First of all, faith counts upon God to do all He has promised, as the only measure of its expectation. It does not rest content with taking some of the promises; it seeks nothing less than to claim every promise that God has made, in its largest and fullest meaning. Under a sense of its own nothingness and utter impotence, it trusts the power of an almighty God to work wonders in the heart in which He dwells.

Faith counts on God with the whole heart and all its strength. Faith yields itself to the promise that God will take full possession of the soul and all through the day and night will inspire its hope and expectation. It recognizes the inseparable link that unites God's promises and His commands, and yields itself to do the one as fully as it trusts the other.

In the pursuit of the power which such a life of faith can give, there is often a faith that seeks and strives but cannot grasp. This is followed by a faith that begins to see that waiting on God is needed, and that quietly rests in the hope of what God will do. This should lead on to an act of decision, in which the soul takes God at His word and claims the fulfillment of the promise, and then looks to Him, even in utter darkness, to perform what He has spoken.

The life of faith to which the abiding presence will be granted surely needs complete mastery of the whole being. Christ's presence actually keeping us all day is a blessed experience and a wonderful privilege. Yet, we must part with much that was formerly thought lawful if He is indeed to be Lord of all, our blessed friend who accompanies us, the joy and light of our life. This faith will be able to claim and to experience the words of the Master: "And surely I will be with you always."

The Practice of the Presence of God

When you practice the presence of God, you will be contented and satisfied, enjoying the treasure of God's presence in your life rather than being in an anxious search for Him.

Do not be content with the little of God's presence you know now. *God has infinite treasure to bestow, and we take up with a little sensible devotion, which passes in a moment.* Blind as we are, we hinder God and stop the current of His graces. But when He finds a soul, penetrated with a lively faith, He pours into it His graces and favors plentifully; there they flow like a torrent, which, after being forcibly stopped against its ordinary course, when it has found a passage, spreads itself with impetuosity and abundance.

Do not stop the torrent of God's graces when He pours them into your soul, but look into your life and break down the bank which hinders His flood of grace into your life. Make way for grace!

Redeem the lost time, for perhaps you have but little left. Death follows us closely, so be well prepared for it. The time presses; there is no room for delay; your soul is at stake.

You must always work at practicing God's presence. Not to advance in the spiritual life is to go backward. Those who have the gale of the Holy Spirit go forward even in sleep. If the vessel of your soul is still tossed with winds and storms, awake to the Lord, who will repose it and quickly calm the sea.

*D*ear Father, thank you for your Word that gives me faith and strengthens my confidence in you. Increase my faith all day long as I consciously rely upon you to give me the strength I need moment by moment. Amen.

We proclaim to you what we have seen and heard, so that you also may have fellowship with us. And our fellowship is with the Father and with his Son, Jesus Christ.

1 John 1:3

21
John's Missionary Message

What a revelation of the call to every witness of the gospel of Jesus Christ! Our message must be nothing less than to proclaim that Christ has opened the way for us simple people to have, day by day, living, loving fellowship with the Father and the Son.

The message suggests to us that the very first duty of the Christian, every day of his life, is to maintain such a close communion with God that he can bear witness to the truth in the fullness of joy. Every day he should be conscious that his life and conversation are proof that his words are true—so true that they appeal with power to the heart. Your life should bear witness to this scriptural truth when you tell others about Christ: "We write this to make our [or your] joy complete" (1 John 1:4).

The substance of the Keswick teaching is this: "A life of communion with God through Christ is a reality to be entered upon, and constantly maintained, by the unconditional and habitual surrender of the whole personality to

Christ's control and government, in the assurance that the living Christ will take possession of the life thus yielded to Him." Such teaching, revealing the infinite claim and power of Christ's love as maintained by the power of the Holy Spirit, will encourage and compel people to make the measure of Christ's surrender for them the only measure of their surrender to Him and His service.

Intimate fellowship with Christ is the secret of daily service and testimony that has the power to make Him known as the deliverer from sin and the inspiration of a life of wholehearted devotion to His service. This intimate and abiding fellowship with Christ secures to us the promise, "And surely I will be with you always." Every Christian needs fellowship with Christ and has a right to claim His presence. By His presence alone will you maintain the spiritual efficiency that will influence the workers and the converts with whom you come in contact.

The Practice of the Presence of God

Recall your first fervor and love for the Lord Jesus Christ. Profit by the example and the sentiments of those who know God in a loving, dear, and intimate way. Pray to Him on your own behalf and on behalf of others who likewise need to know Him.

When you surrender yourself to the service of Christ, make the sacrifice of yourself to Him in view of His love alone. Firmly resolve to be wholly devoted to Him. Pray in this regard for others who are committing their lives to follow the Lord as His faithful disciples.

For the right practice of the presence of God, your heart

must be empty of all other things, because God will possess only the empty heart. He cannot act in your heart and do what He pleases there unless you leave it vacant to Him.

Nothing in the world is more sweet and delightful than the kind of life that is in continual conversation with God. Only those who practice and experience this can comprehend what I mean. Yet, I do not advise you to practice conversation with God from that motive! Do not simply seek the pleasure which this experience provides. Have conversation with God from a principle of love and because God desires to have such fellowship with you.

If you are a preacher, above all other things preach the practice of the presence of God. If you can advise others in their spiritual lives, advise all the world to practice His presence. To do so is necessary, and easy.

*D*ear Father God, you graciously sent your Son into the world to establish a personal relationship with us, to call out a people from the world to be companions of both you and your Son. Thank you for sharing your great love. Thank you for redeeming me from sin and death so I could have lasting fellowship with you. I empty my heart of everything that is unworthy of your presence, and pray you would be my personal advisor all the day for Jesus' sake. Amen.

The mystery that has been kept hidden for ages and generations, but is now disclosed to the saints . . . the glorious riches of this mystery, which is Christ in you, the hope of glory.

Colossians 1:26, 27

22
Paul's Missionary Message

Paul believed the very center and substance of his gospel was the indwelling Christ. He spoke of the "glorious riches of this mystery, which is Christ in you, the hope of glory." Though he had preached this gospel for many years, he still asked for prayer so God might enable him to make known that mystery rightly (Col. 4:2–4).

Many complain with regard to older churches that after a time there appears to be no further growth, and very little of the joy and power for bearing witness to Christ Jesus. The question comes whether the church is living in the experience of the indwelling Christ, so that the sons and daughters whom she sends out know the secret, and make it the substance of their witnessing, teaching and preaching.

Some years ago one of our ministers went to the foreign mission field to do deputation work. Before he left, there was a little gathering for prayer, where he asked what his message should be. The thought was expressed that in speaking to Christians, he should press home to them a message of a full salvation, and rouse their hearts to believe in and accept an indwelling Christ. On his return he told with what deep interest the presentation of this truth had been received, many saying that they had never before understood this rightly.

Dr. Maclaren said years ago that it seemed as if the Church had lost the truth of the indwelling Christ.[1] We speak of Paul's missionary methods, but is there not a greater need of Paul's missionary message, as it culminates in these supreme words: "Christ in you, the hope of glory"? Paul felt the need of much prayer to enable him to give the message rightly. Is there not a call to all intercessors, and to our beloved ministers and missionaries themselves, to make it a matter of first importance to obtain the power, and from a living experience to lead Christians into the enjoyment of their rightful heritage? "Jesus replied, 'If anyone loves me, he will obey my teaching. My Father will love him, and we will come to him and make our home with him' " (John 14:23). Pray that the Church will share in the blessing, be restored to its rightful place, and proclaim this truth: "Christ in you, the hope of glory."

The Practice of the Presence of God

Remember the great need you have of the grace and assistance of God. You should never lose sight of Him—not for a moment.

Make immediately a holy and firm resolution to never for-

[1]Alexander Maclaren (1826–1910) was a Scottish minister known for his expository preaching, and the first president of the Baptist World Alliance in 1905.

get Him willfully, but to spend the rest of your days in His sacred presence, and if He thinks fit, deprived, for the love of Him, of all consolations.

Heartily involve yourself in the practice of His presence, and if you do as you ought, you will soon find the effects of it.

I cannot imagine how believers can be satisfied without the practice of the presence of God. Keep yourself with Him in the center of your soul as much as you can.

While you are with God, fear nothing; and do not turn from Him, for this is unbearable and unjustifiable.

*D*ear Father, help me to know your Son, as an indwelling Lord and Savior, more than I do at this present time. Help me to know Him better than the early disciples. I pray that your Holy Spirit would give me great insight into His indwelling character as I read your Word. Amen.

You are witnesses, and so is God, of how holy, righteous and blameless we were among you who believed.

1 Thessalonians 2:10

23
The Missionary's Life

More than once Paul appealed to what his converts had seen of his own life. For example, he wrote to the Corinthians: "Now this is our boast: Our conscience testifies that we have conducted ourselves in the world, and especially in our relations with you, in the holiness and sincerity that are from God. We have done so not according to worldly wisdom but according to God's grace" (2 Cor. 1:12, 13). Christ taught His disciples as much by His life as by His teaching. Paul sought to be a living witness to the truth of all that he preached about Christ: that Christ was able to save and to keep from sin by renewing the whole nature through the power of His Holy Spirit, by Christ himself becoming the life of those who believe in Him.

Far too often we have hidden Christ, whom we are giving our lives to reveal. Only in proportion as we can manifest the character of Christ in and through our own lives can we gain a hearing for the gospel. Only as far as we can live Christ before the eyes of others can we help them to understand His message.

See how Paul's appeal to his life as holy and righteous and blameless gave him courage to put a high standard before his converts. In the same epistle he calls them to trust God, to establish their hearts blameless in holiness before Him, praying, "May he strengthen your hearts so that you will be blameless and holy in the presence of our God and Father when our Lord Jesus comes with all his holy ones" (1 Thess. 3:13). Later in the epistle he prayed again, "May God himself, the God of peace, sanctify you through and through. May your whole spirit, soul and body be kept blameless at the coming of our Lord Jesus Christ. The one who calls you is faithful and he will do it" (1 Thess. 5:23, 24).

In Phil. 4:9, he wrote, "Whatever you have learned or received or heard from me, or seen in me—put it into practice. And the God of peace will be with you." And in 1 Tim. 1:14–16, he wrote, "The grace of our Lord was poured out on me abundantly, along with the faith and love that are in Christ Jesus. Here is a trustworthy saying that deserves full acceptance: Christ Jesus came into the world to save sinners—of whom I am the worst. But for that very reason I was shown mercy so that in me, the worst of sinners, Christ Jesus might display his unlimited patience as an example for those who would believe on him and receive eternal life." Let us believe that when Paul said, "Christ lives in me," "I live no more," he spoke of an actual, divine, unceasing abiding of Christ in him, working in him from hour to hour all that was well-pleasing to the Father. And let us not rest until we can say, "The Christ of Paul is my Christ! His enduement is mine too."

The Practice of the Presence of God

The practice of the presence of God will not bring much fatigue to your body. However, it is proper sometimes to deprive your body of many little pleasures that are innocent and lawful. It is more than reasonable to expect that God will not permit you to take greater delight in other pleasures than the delight of being entirely devoted to Him.

Do not put any violent constraint upon yourself and think that this is the way to practice His presence.

You must serve God in a holy freedom by doing your business faithfully without any trouble or nervousness.

Whenever you find your mind wandering from God, recall your mind sweetly back to God with tranquillity of soul.

To practice the presence of God in your life, you must put your whole trust in Him, laying aside all other cares, even some particular forms of devotion which have become an end in themselves rather than the means to exercise the presence of God.

*D*ear God, I desire to live a holy, blameless and righteous life in Jesus Christ, allowing His life to be lived in and through me, so others might come to accept the truth of His gospel and invite Him into their lives as a living and abiding presence. Help me, Father, to do your will, and be present with me all the day. Amen.

He [the Spirit of truth] will bring glory to me by taking from what is mine and making it known to you.

John 16:14

24
The Holy Spirit

When our Lord said to His disciples, "And surely I will be with you always," they did not at first understand or experience the full meaning of those words.

At Pentecost they were filled with the Holy Spirit and that Spirit from heaven brought down into their hearts the glorified Lord Jesus, and they began their new life in the joy of the abiding presence.

All our attempts to claim to live that life of continuous, unbroken communion will be in vain unless we too yield ourselves wholly to the power and the indwelling of the ever-blessed Spirit.

Throughout the Church of Christ a lack of faith is apparent regarding the Spirit as God, about what He can enable us to be, and about how completely He demands full and undisturbed possession of our whole being. All our faith in the fulfillment of Christ's glorious promises of the Father and the Son making their home in us is subject to the one essential and indispensable condition—a life utterly and unceasingly yielded to the rule and leading of the Spirit of Christ.

Let no one say, "The experience of Christ's being with us every day and all the day is impossible." Christ meant His Word to be a simple and eternal reality. He meant the promises to be accepted: "Whoever has my commands and obeys them, he is the one who loves me. He who loves me will be loved by my Father, and I too will love him and show myself to him," and "we will come to him and make our home with him" (John 14:21, 23). His promises are absolute divine truth. But this truth could be experienced only where the Spirit, in His power as God, was known and believed in and obeyed. What Christ spoke of in John 14, Paul testified to when he said, "Christ lives in me." Or, as John expressed it, "Those who obey his commands live in him, and he in them. And this is how we know that he lives in us: We know it by the Spirit he gave us" (1 John 3:24).

Christ came as God to make known the Father, and the Spirit came as God to make known the Son in us. We need to understand that the Spirit is God and claims absolute subjection. He is willing to take possession of our whole being and enable us to fulfill all that Christ asks of us. The Spirit can deliver us from all the power of the flesh, and He can conquer the power of the world. The Spirit, through whom Christ Jesus will manifest himself to us, is nothing less than His abiding presence: "And surely I will be with you always, to the very end of the age" (Matt. 28:20).

The Practice of the Presence of God

The purpose of your life is to be with God. You may continue with Him in a conversation of love, persevering in His holy presence, by acts of praise, adoration or desire for Him. At other times you will be in His presence through acts of resignation and submission as well as thanksgiving. Look for ways the Spirit would have you be in His presence.

Do not be discouraged when you become disgusted with your human nature, but subject your body to the obedience of Christ.

Resolve to seek Christ and walk in His presence even unto death. Persevere, regardless of all the difficulties that will occur.

Christ requires you to remember Him, adore Him, pray for His grace, offer Him your sufferings, give thanks for His favors. In the midst of your troubles, console yourself with Him as often as you can. Lift up your heart to Him at meals and when you are in the company of others. Every time you remember Him, it will be acceptable to Him.

You do not need to come to God with loud crying. He is nearer to you than you are aware of.

*A*lmighty God, thank you for the truths you have taught me in your Word, the Bible. Through your Word, I know that you are one God in three Persons: Father, Son, and Holy Spirit. Thank you for being present with me at each moment of the day. Thank you for living in my life in such a way that through the indwelling Holy Spirit, I am continually in the presence of the Father and the Son. Amen.

Be filled with the Spirit. Speak to one another with psalms, hymns and spiritual songs. Sing and make music in your heart to the Lord, always giving thanks to God the Father for everything

. . .

Ephesians 5:18–20

25

Filled With the Spirit

If the expression "filled with the Spirit" pertained only to the story of Pentecost, we might naturally think that it was something special and not meant for ordinary life. But our text teaches us the great lesson that it is meant for every Christian and for everyday life.

To realize this more fully, think of what the Holy Spirit was in Christ Jesus and under what conditions He, as man, was filled with the Spirit. He received the Spirit when He was praying, and He yielded himself as a sacrifice to God in going down into the sinner's baptism. Full of the Holy Spirit, He was led to the forty days of fasting, sacrificing the needs of His body to be free for fellowship with the Father and the victory over Satan. He even refused, when He was hungry, to listen to the temptation of the Evil One to use His power to make bread to supply His hunger. He was led by the Spirit all through life until He, by the eternal Spirit, offered himself without blemish unto God. In Christ, the Spirit meant prayer, obedience, and sacrifice.

Even so we, if we are to follow Christ, to have His

mind in us, to live out His life, we must seek to regard the fullness of the Spirit as a daily supply, a daily provision. If we are to live the life of obedience, of joy, of self-sacrifice, and of power for service, we must be filled with the Spirit. There may be occasions when that fullness of the Spirit will become especially manifested to us. But every day and all the day it is only as we are led by the Spirit that we can abide in Christ Jesus, conquer the flesh and the world, live our life with God in prayer, and live with our fellow man in humble, holy, fruitful service.

Above all, only when we are filled with the Spirit can these words of Jesus be fully understood and experienced: "And surely I will be with you always." Let no one think this is too high, that this is impossible. What is impossible with us is possible with God! And if we cannot attain to it at once, let us at least make it, in an act of holy decision, our definite aim, our unceasing prayer, our childlike expectation. "I will be with you always" was meant for daily life, but only with the sure and all-sufficient aid of that blessed Spirit of whom Jesus said, "Whoever believes in me, as the Scripture has said, streams of living water will flow from within him" (John 7:38). Our faith in Christ will be the measure of our fullness of the Spirit. The measure of the power of the Spirit in us will be the measure of our experience in the presence of Christ.

The Practice of the Presence of God

You can be with God even when you are not at church. You may talk with Him in your heart, whenever you retire from time to time to converse with Him in meekness, humility and love.

Everyone is capable of familiar conversation with God—some more, some less. He knows what you can do. Begin then.

Perhaps God expects you to make but one generous resolution. Have courage. You have but little time to live: live and die with God.

Suffering will be sweet and pleasant to you while you are with God. However, the greatest pleasures will be as cruel punishments to you if you are without Him.

Become accustomed to worship Him by degrees, to beg Him for His grace. Offer God your heart from time to time in the midst of your business, even every moment if you can. Do not confine yourself to certain rules or particular forms of devotion, but act always with a general confidence in God and with love and humility.

*D*ear Father, thank you for promising me that by your grace and through faith in your Son, I might be cleansed from my sins and filled with your Spirit. I intend to obey you in everything as I prayerfully read the Scriptures and seek your will; empower me by your Spirit to do so! Amen.

Christ lives in me. When Christ, who is your life, appears, then you also will appear with him in glory.

Galatians 2:20; Colossians 3:4

26
The Christ Life

Christ's life was more than His teaching, more than His work, more even than His death. It was His life in the sight of God and man that gave value to what He said and did and suffered. And it is this life, glorified in the resurrection, that He imparts to His people, enabling them to live out the Christ life before others.

"All men will know that you are my disciples if you love one another" (John 13:35). Life in the new brotherhood of the Holy Spirit made both Jews and Greeks feel there was some superhuman power about Christ's disciples. They gave living proof of the truth of what they said, that God's love had come down and taken possession of them.

Unless the Christian lives out the Christ life on an entirely different level from that on which other men live, he misses the deepest secret of power and success in his work. When Christ sent His disciples forth, it was with the command: "Stay in the city until you have been clothed with power from on high" (Luke 24:49). And again He said, "But you will receive power when the Holy Spirit comes on you; and you will be my witnesses in Jerusalem, and in all Judea and Samaria, and to the ends of the earth" (Acts 1:8). Many have felt that it is not learning, not zeal, and not the willingness for self-sacrifice in Christ's service, but the secret experience of the life hidden with Christ in God that enables him to meet and overcome every difficulty.

Everything depends upon your life with God in Christ being right. It was so with Christ, with the disciples, with Paul. It is the simplicity and intensity of our life in Christ Jesus, and of the life of Christ Jesus in us, that sustains us in the daily drudgery of work, that makes us conquerors over self and everything that could hinder the Christ life, and gives the victory over the powers of evil and over the hearts from which the evil spirits have been cast out.

Life in the Spirit is everything. It was so in Christ Jesus. It must be so in His servants. It can be so, because Christ himself will live in us. When He spoke the words, "And surely I will be with you always," He meant nothing less than this: "Every day and all the day I am with you, the secret of your life, your joy, and your strength."

Oh, to learn what hidden treasures are contained in the blessed words we love to repeat: "I will be with you always."

The Practice of the Presence of God

Our minds are extremely roving. When your mind has contracted bad habits of wandering and dissipation, these are difficult to overcome, and commonly draw us against our wills to the things of the earth. But your will is master of all your faculties. Your will must recall your thoughts back to God as their supreme end.

One remedy for a wandering mind is to confess your faults and humble yourself before God. Use only a few words in your prayers, since long discourses in prayer are often the occasion for wandering.

Hold yourself in prayer before God like a paralytic beggar at a rich man's gate. Let it be your business to keep your mind in the presence of the Lord.

Do not become troubled or disquieted over wandering thoughts, since this will further distract your mind. Your will must bring your mind back to tranquillity. If you persevere in this manner, God himself will help you.

When you keep your mind strictly in the presence of God and become accustomed to think of Him often, you will find it easy to keep your mind calm in the time of prayer, or at least recall it from its wanderings. There are great advantages in the practice of the presence of God. Set about it seriously!

*D*ear Jesus, thank you for not leaving me to my own thoughts and devices as I seek to be consciously with you every day. Thank you for making your life in me; however, help me to never take your presence in my life for granted. Help me to experience a deeper closeness with you. Amen.

Your attitude should be the same as that of Christ Jesus.

Philippians 2:5

27
The Christlike Life

What was the attitude that was in Christ Jesus? Paul wrote, "Being in very nature God . . . [He] made himself nothing, taking the very nature of a servant, being made in human likeness . . . he humbled himself and became obedient to death—even death on a cross" (Phil. 2:6–8). Self-emptying and self-sacrifice, obedience to God's will, love to men, even unto the death of the cross, such was the character of Christ for which God so highly exalted Him. Such is the character of Christ that we are to imitate. He was made in our likeness so we might be conformed to the likeness of God.

Self-effacement, self-sacrifice that God's will might be done and that man might be saved—such was the life of Christ. Love is not self-seeking. This was His life: He lived only to please God and to bless us.

Let no one say that this is an impossibility. Whatever is impossible with us is possible with God. We are called to work out a Christlike character with fear and trembling: "For it is God who works in you to will and to act according to his good purpose" (Phil. 2:13). And Jesus said of himself, “It is the Father, living in me, who is doing his work” (John 14:10).

The Christian who is to commend the gospel must first embody it in a character fully conformed to the likeness of Jesus Christ. Only as far as we can live Christ before the eyes of others can we help them to understand His message.

Only as the Church aims at making some marked degree of likeness to Christ’s character the standard for Christian conduct will we be able to pass this on to converts and say to them “Be ye followers of us, even as we are of Christ.”

Let us not rest until our faith lays hold of the promise: “It is God who works in us.” Our confidence must be aroused to claim the promise that since we are called to reveal the character of Christ, so the power will be given by Christ to fulfill this high and holy calling. Let every Christian make this his one great plea and aim: to have the mind that was in Christ Jesus.

The Practice of the Presence of God

You ought to help others by your advice, and yet more by your good example. Your only business in this life is to please God; anything else is folly and vanity. Employ your life in loving and serving God, who by His mercy has called you for that very purpose. God incessantly bestows upon you great favors. Make good use of them for others as well as yourself.

Return with full assurance to the Father of mercies, who is always ready to receive you affectionately. For the love of God, renounce everything that is not of Him. He deserves infinitely more. Think of Him without ceasing. Put all your trust in Him. You will soon find the effects of this in receiving the abundance of His grace, with which you can do all things, and without which you can do nothing but sin.

You will not escape the dangers which abound in life without the actual and *continual* help of God. Pray to Him for it *continually*. But how can you pray to Him without being with Him? How can you be with Him without thinking of Him often? And how can you think of Him often unless you make this a holy habit?

You must *know* before you can *love*. In order to *know* God, you must *think* of Him often; and when you come to *love* Him, you shall then also *think* of Him often, for your heart will be with your treasure.

Should you have material misfortunes, take advantage of them by placing all your confidence in God. God will give you powerful friends inclined to help you. But do not allow your love for your friends to encroach upon the love due to God.

*D*ear God, I want to have the character of Jesus Christ; His loving, gentle spirit that sought both justice and mercy in every relationship and in every situation. Help me to be so Christlike that others will see the Spirit of your Son shining forth out of my life, and because of the work that He can do, come to submit their lives to Him. Amen.

Come near to God and he will come near to you.

James 4:8

28

Christ, the Nearness of God

The holiness of God is the union of God's infinite distance from sinful man with God's infinite nearness in His redeeming grace. Faith must ever seek to realize both the distance and the nearness.

In Christ God has come near, so very near to us, and now the command comes: If you would have God come still nearer, you must come near to Him. The promised nearness of Christ Jesus expressed in the promise, "And surely I will be with you always," can be experienced only as we come near to Him.

First of all, draw near to Him at the beginning of each day. Yield yourself to Him anew for His holy presence to rest upon uou. Voluntarily, intentionally, and wholeheartedly turn away from the world and wait on God to make himself known to your soul. Give time and all your heart and strength to allow Him to reveal himself. It is impossible to expect the abiding presence of Christ with us through the day unless there is the definite daily exercise of strong desire to be with Him and childlike trust in His word: "Come near to God and he will come near to you."

Second, make a simple childlike offering of yourself and your life to do His will alone in everything, and seek above everything else to please Him. His promise is sure: "If anyone loves me, he will obey my teaching. My Father will love him, and we will come to him and make our home with him" (John 14:23).

Then comes the quiet assurance of faith that God is with us, even if there is not much feeling or sense of His presence. We also are assured that as we go out to do His will, He will watch over us, keep us, and, what is more, strengthen us in the inner man with divine strength for the work we have to do for Him.

Child of God, let these words come to you with a new meaning each morning: "Come near to God and he will come near to you." Wait patiently and He will speak in divine power: "And surely I will be with you always."

The Practice of the Presence of God

Think often on God by day and by night, in your business and in your recreation. He is always near you and with you; do not leave Him alone. You would think it rude to leave a friend alone who came to visit you; why then must God be neglected? Do not forget Him, but think on Him often. Adore Him continually, live and die with Him: this is the glorious business of the Christian. If you do not know this business, then you must learn it.

Sometimes you will be led to *not* pray for someone to be delivered from their pains. But you can pray earnestly that God would give them strength and patience to bear them for as long as He pleases. Comfort others by reminding them of their God, who holds them fastened to the cross, and who will release them when He thinks fit. Happy are those who suffer with Him! Pain can come as a favor from God, as a means He employs for their salvation.

Convince yourself that God is often (in some sense) nearer to us and more effectually present with us in sickness than in health. Put your trust in God in sickness and in health.

When afflictions come from God, only He can cure them. He may send diseases of the body to cure those of the soul. Comfort yourself with the Sovereign Physician of both the body and the soul.

Pains and sufferings can be a paradise to you while you suffer with your God, and the greatest pleasures could be hell to you if you relish them without Him. All your consolation can come from knowing that you are suffering something for His sake. See Him by *faith*; see Him in such a manner that you may say sometimes, "*My faith is weak, but I see.*" Continue with God as your support and comfort.

Dear Father, I come before you aware of my unworthiness and thankful that you have bid me to come near to you. Apart from the willing sacrifice of your Son, I could not come near you, and so I thank you for providing the way for me to come into your presence. In sickness and in health, I know you are with me. Help me to learn from my afflictions, knowing that they come with your kind permission. Amen.

Having loved his own who were in the world, he [Jesus] now showed them the full extent of his love.

John 13:1

29
Love

These are the opening words of that holy confidential talk of Jesus with His disciples, as out of the depths of eternity He talked with them in the last hours before He went to Gethsemane (John 13—17). They are the revelation and full display of that divine love which was manifested in His death on the cross.

He begins with the new commandment: "Love one another. As I have loved you, so you must love one another" (John 13:34). A little later follows: "If you love me, you will obey what I command. . . . He who loves me will be loved by my Father, and I too will love him and show myself to him. . . . And we will come to him and make our home with him" (John 14:15, 21, 23).

The new life, the heavenly life in Christ Jesus, is to be the unfolding of God's love in Christ. Farther on He said, "As the Father has loved me, so have I loved you. Now remain in my love. If you obey my commands, you will remain in my love, just as I have obeyed my Father's commands and remain in his love. I have told you this so that my joy may be in you and that your joy may be complete.

My command is this: Love each other as I have loved you. Greater love has no one than this, that one lay down his life for his friends" (John 15:9–13). And later He prayed, "May they be brought to complete unity to let the world know that you sent me and have loved them even as you have loved me. . . . I have made you known to them, and will continue to make you known in order that the love you have for me may be in them and that I myself may be in them" (John 17:23, 26).

Can it be stated any plainer that God's love to Christ is given to pass into us and to become our life, that the love wherewith the Father loved the Son is to be in us? If the Lord Jesus is to show himself to us, He can do it only to the loving heart. If we are to claim His daily presence with us, it can only be as a relationship of infinite tender love between Him and us, love rooted in the faith of God's love to Christ coming into our hearts, and showing itself in obedience to His commandments and in love to one another.

We see how in the early church the first love was forsaken after a time, and confidence was put in all the activities of service (Rev. 2–4).

It is only in the atmosphere of a holy living love that the abiding presence of the loving Christ can be known, and the depth of the divine love expressed in Christ's promise "And surely I will be with you always," will be realized.

The Practice of the Presence of God

Many bodily diseases would be much alleviated if we were well accustomed to the exercise of the presence of God. God often permits us to suffer a little to purify our souls and to oblige us to continue with Him. Your pains can be proofs of God's love toward you.

Pray to God for strength to endure your pains. Adore Him in your infirmities. Ask Him humbly and affectionately (as a child his father) to make you conformable to His holy will. Make a virtue out of your extremity. Ask God to give you the strength to bear resolutely, for the love of Him, all that He should please for as long as He shall please.

God has many ways of drawing you to himself. He will sometimes hide himself from you; but *faith* alone, which will not fail you in time of need, ought to be your support and the foundation of your confidence which must be in God.

Though all the world is suffering, in the presence of God you may always be happy and feel joy so continual and so great that you will scarcely contain them.

Faith will give you a strong conviction that He never forsakes us until we have first forsaken Him. Fear to leave Him! Be always with Him! Live and die in His presence!

Dear Father, I remember how your Son Jesus was obedient unto death and how He endured the pain and disgrace of the cross for me. In everything I resolve to be obedient to you because I love you so much. Help me to love others as you have loved me so I can lead them to accept Jesus as their Lord and Savior. Whenever I have to endure pain and suffering, help me to increase my faith and trust in you. Help me to build Christian character even in pain. Amen.

"If you can?" said Jesus. "Everything is possible for him who believes." Immediately the boy's father exclaimed, "I do believe; help me overcome my unbelief!"

Mark 9:23, 24

30

The Trial and Triumph of Faith

What a glorious promise: "Everything is possible for him who believes!" And yet, the greatness of the promise constitutes the trial of faith. At first we do not really believe it is true. But when we have grasped it, then comes the real trial in the thought: "Such a wonder-working faith is utterly beyond my reach."

But what constitutes the trial of faith soon becomes its triumph. How can this be? When Christ said to the father of the child, "Everything is possible for him who believes," the father felt that this was only casting him into deeper despair. How could his faith be able to work the miracle? But as he looked into the face of Christ, and the love of the tender eye touched his heart, he felt sure that this blessed Man not only had the power to heal his child but also the power to inspire him with the needed faith. The impression Christ produced upon him made not only the one miracle of the healing possible, but also the second miracle that he should have so great a faith. And with tears he cried, "I do believe; help me overcome my unbelief." The very greatness of faith's trial was the greatness of faith's triumph.

What a lesson! Of all things that are possible to faith, the most impossible is that I should be able to exercise such faith. The abiding presence of Christ is possible to faith. And this faith is possible to the soul that clings to Christ and trusts Him. As surely as He will lead us into His abiding presence all the day, so surely will He strengthen us with divine power for the faith that claims and receives the promise. Blessed is the hour when the believer sees how entirely he is dependent on Christ for the faith as well as the blessing, and, in the consciousness of the unbelief that is still struggling within, he casts himself on the power and the love of Jesus: "I do believe; help me overcome my unbelief."

Through such trial and triumph, sometimes the triumph of despair, we enter upon our inheritance—the abiding presence of Him who speaks to us now: "And surely I will be with you always." Let us wait at His feet until we know that He has blessed us: "I can do everything through him who gives me strength" (Phil. 4:13).

The Practice of the Presence of God

Prayers of total surrender to God regardless of the circumstances are difficult but most acceptable to Him and sweet to those who love Him. Love sweetens pain and affliction, and when you love God, you will suffer for His sake with joy and courage.

Comfort yourself with Him, who is the only physician of all our maladies. He is the Father of the afflicted, always ready to help us. He loves us infinitely more than we imagine. Love Him, and do not seek consolation elsewhere.

When you are close to death, if you have practiced the presence of God, you will be very satisfied. You may choose not to pray for relief but for strength to suffer with courage, humility and love. Ah, how sweet it is to suffer with God!

However great your sufferings may be, receive them with love. It is paradise to suffer and be with Him. In this life, if we would enjoy the peace of paradise, we must accustom ourselves to a familiar, humble, affectionate conversation with God. Make your heart a spiritual temple, wherein you adore Him incessantly. Do not think or say anything that may displease Him. When your mind is adoring God, suffering will become full of unction and consolation.

To arrive at a state of practicing the presence of God is very difficult in the beginning, for you must act purely in faith. But you can do all things with the grace of God, which He never refuses to those who ask it earnestly. Knock, persevere in knocking, and He will open to you in His due time and grant you all at once what He has deferred during many years.

*D*ear Father, when I think of the close relationship that Murray and Lawrence had with you, I pray that you would increase my belief to know you as well as they did. Amen.

Now to him who is able to do immeasurably more than all we ask or imagine, according to his power that is at work within us, to him be glory in the church and in Christ Jesus throughout all generations, for ever and ever! Amen.

Ephesians 3:20, 21

31
Immeasurably More

In the great prayers of Paul, he apparently reached the highest expressions possible of the life to which God's mighty power could bring the believer. But Paul is not content. In this doxology he rises still higher and lifts us up to give glory to God as "able to do immeasurably more than all we ask or imagine." Pause a moment to think what that "immeasurably more" means.

Think of the words, "very great and precious promises" (2 Pet. 1:4). Think of "his incomparably great power for us who believe. That power is like the working of his mighty strength, which he exerted in Christ when he raised him from the dead and seated him at his right hand in the heavenly realms" (Eph. 1:19, 20). Think of the grace of our Lord as immeasurably more with faith and love, which is in Christ Jesus, so that where sin abounded grace did abound more exceedingly. He lifts our hearts to give glory to God as able to do "immeasurably more than all we ask or imagine," according to the greatness of that power which works in us; nothing less than the exceeding greatness of the power that raised Christ from the dead.

And as our hearts begin to feel that there is here a prospect of something God will work in us beyond all our imagination, He lifts our hearts to join in the universal chorus: "To him be glory in the church and in Christ Jesus throughout all generations, for ever and ever! Amen."

As we worship and adore, the call comes to believe in this almighty God, who is working in our hearts, according to His mighty power, able and willing to fulfill every one of His exceeding great and precious promises, and, where sin abounded, to prove that grace abounds more exceedingly.

Paul began his great prayer, "I kneel before the Father" (Eph. 3:14). He ended it by bringing us to our knees, to give glory to Him as able to fulfill every promise, to reveal Christ dwelling in our hearts, and keep us in the life of love that leads to being filled with all the fullness of God.

Child of God, bow in deep adoration, giving glory to God, until your heart learns to believe: the prayer *will* be fulfilled. Jesus Christ will dwell in your heart by faith. Faith in this almighty God, and the exceeding abundance of His grace and power, will teach you that the abiding indwelling of Christ in the heart is the secret of the abiding presence.

The Practice of the Presence of God

God knows what is best for you, and everything He does is for your good. When you know how much He loves you, you should always be ready to receive equally and without concern anything sweet or bitter from His hand. Everything that comes from Him should please you.

The worst afflictions never appear intolerable, unless we

see them in the wrong light. If we see them as permitted by God or dispensed from His hand, we know that it is from our loving Father, and our sufferings will lose their bitterness and become a matter of consolation.

Let your primary business be to *know* God. The more you know God, the more you will desire to know Him. *Knowledge* of God is commonly a measure of *love*. The deeper and more extensive your *knowledge*, the greater will be your *love*.

Do not be content with loving God for the mere favors He gives. Such favors cannot bring us so near to Him as faith does by one simple act. Seek Him often by faith! Seek Him within you.

Be devoted to Him in good earnest. Love Him supremely. If we do what we can on our part, we shall soon see that change in us which we seek.

*T*hank you, Father, for working in my life in ways immeasurably greater than I would ever have thought or imagined possible. Your love overwhelms me as I think of the opportunities you have given me to serve you and others. I do not deserve these opportunities, and it is only by your grace that I have been able to bring some blessing to others. Continue with me each day. Amen.